The Caring Person's Illness

DANIEL T. BUDENZ, Ph. D.

CompCare Publishers
2415 Annapolis Lane
Minneapolis, Minnesota 55441

Library of Congress Cataloging-in-Publication Data

Budenz, Daniel T., 1950-
    The Caring Person's Illness/Daniel T. Budenz.
    p. cm.
    ISBN 0-89638-214-1
    1. Co-dependence (Psychology) I. Title.
RC569.5.C63B83 1990   90-1408
616.86—dc20   CIP

Cover design by Susan Rinek

Originally published as Affected Family Member Syndrome
© Dr. Daniel T. Budenz, 1979, 1980, 1988.

Inquiries, orders, and catalog requests should be addressed to:
CompCare Publishers
2415 Annapolis Lane
Minneapolis, MN 55441
Call toll free 800/328-3330
Minnesota residents 612/559-4800

  5   4   3   2   1
 94   93   92   91   90

Acknowledgments

The author recognizes with special gratitude Richard B. Weedman, M.S.S.W., Penny Clemens, Ph.D., and the Grant Hospital Team for his early instruction (1970-1972) in the disease process of alcoholism and in relapse intervention and prevention techniques.

This book is dedicated to you and other families with the courage to change!

I am extremely grateful for the opportunity over the past twenty years to serve families suffering from the effects of one or more generations of alcoholism/chemical dependency.

Most of those twenty years were spent in a hospital environment. In those hospitals, I have seen many types of illness and disease. However, I know of no disease that so thoroughly devastates the family and leaves longer-lasting scars than chemical dependency. I also know the great courage families have shown in standing up to this frightening disease. It is to you who possess that family courage that I dedicate this booklet.

Introduction

There is a disease that affects millions. It is a highly treatable disease, and yet many never recognize they have it or seek help.

This disease has identifiable symptoms, causes an individual physical, emotional, and spiritual pain, worsens with time, and usually harms those around him or her. Tragically, many people with this disease suffer for years and, as a result, also pass the disease on to their children.

Perhaps you've never heard its name before. But, as you learn about it in this booklet, you may find that you, too, have struggled with this illness.

The name of the disease is Affected Family Member Syndrome (AFMS), also known as codependency. It affects four times as many persons as alcoholism or drug addiction. In fact, Affected Family Member Syndrome is often a contributing factor to a person's becoming alcohol- or drug-dependent.

Initially it may feel uncomfortable for you, the family member of a chemically dependent person, to think of your own problem as a primary, physical disease. You may prefer simply to think of your problem as a set of emotions and behaviors that frequently, if not always, occur in people who live with a chemically dependent person. It would be most unfortunate if the word *disease* were to prevent readers from benefiting from the other information in this booklet. There is increasing neurochemical evidence to support the idea that AFMS is, in fact, a disease. My primary point, however, is not that AFMS or codependency must be *called* a disease, but that it needs to be *treated* as a disease. Why? Because years of experience have shown that treating AFMS as a disease helps affected family members *get better*—physically, emotionally, and spiritually.

The model of chemical dependency used in some medical and hospital settings concentrates on the immediate problems presented by the addict or closely related problems associated with the addict's chief complaint or obvious condition. However, many of us in the treatment field prefer to view chemical dependency as a *family* disease. I have developed a prevention-oriented, whole-family approach to the disease that I call the California Model. The California Model seriously addresses the addict's condition, but puts a *primary* focus on whole-family assessment; we attempt to prevent or intervene in family problems that may be contributing to the addict's problems. Again, we use this approach because it works; it helps the entire family get better.

The term I use for the family disease of alcoholism/chemical dependency is Affected Family Syndrome, or AFS. AFS comprises three primary patient groups: (1) victims of Fetal Alcohol Syndrome, (2) chemically dependent persons, and (3) affected family members, also called codependents. I call the illness of affected family members Affected Family Member Syndrome, or AFMS. The affected family members, or codependents, probably are the most often misdiagnosed.

This booklet is for people who are suffering from AFMS. (For your review, the California Model as it applies to Addiction Recovery is presented in chart form on page 49.) If you would like a brief definition of the other two illnesses, Fetal Alcohol Syndrome and chemical dependency, please see the appendix.

This booklet is presented in a question-and-answer format to allow you to follow the main concepts and/or skip sections as you desire.

Q: What is the definition of *disease?*

A: Perhaps this definition from an older copy of *Webster's* says it best:

Disease: 1. Trouble.

The new *Webster's* defines *disease* as follows:

Disease: 1. An abnormal condition of an organism or part that impairs normal physiological functioning, especially as a result of infection, inherent weakness, or environmental stress.

2. A condition or tendency as of society, regarded as abnormal and harmful.

3. Lack of ease.

All three of these definitions describe the situation of family members of chemically dependent people. I stress this, because the problems of affected family members are *not* secondary to the problems of the chemically dependent person. Affected family members require primary attention and focus just as chemically dependent people do.

Q: What is Affected Family Member Syndrome?

A: Affected Family Member Syndrome is a primary illness related to, but separate from, chemical dependency.

It is a physical as well as psychological reaction to the stress of coping with a chemically dependent person's alcohol- or drug-induced behavior.

The illness is characterized by an accumulation of unexpressed feelings: *guilt, shame, self-pity, anger, resentment, and worry.* These are known as the "intoxicant emotions" of the disease. It is also characterized by a strong need to control oneself, others, and family situations. A wide range of physical symptoms and complications are often present. The symptoms are progressive and often continue in spite of the fact that the addict may be recovering—or may no longer even be present in the family.

It is important to understand what AFMS is not. It is not a moral problem. It is not caused by "weak character." It usually has nothing to do with neurochemical disorders like schizophrenia or manic depression. In the early phases, the actions and attitudes of family members are perfectly rational and understandable. These people are simply trying to help a loved one. Family members show a lot of moral courage as they try to help one another. In the later phases of the disease, behaviors surface which may appear to indicate a personality disorder or mental illness—for example, depression or anxiety. However, once the affected family member is in treatment for AFMS, these symptoms can be arrested.

Once treated and arrested, this illness has strong tendencies toward relapse.

Q: Who is an affected family member?

A: Anyone who grew up with, at one time lived with, or is now in a household with a chemically dependent person and, as a result, experiences continued and growing problems in any area of life.

For example, you may now be, or once were, married to someone who drinks too much or uses drugs. You may be the adult child of an alcohol or substance abuser. Sisters, brothers, and even close friends of the chemically dependent are affected family members if they experience continued and growing problems.

You may be a recovering chemically dependent person and, at the same time, the child or spouse of an alcohol or substance abuser, and were never treated for this other disease, AFMS.

To help you determine if you are an affected family member, ask yourself the following sixteen questions:

1. Do I sometimes lose sleep because of worrying about the person in my family who abuses alcohol or drugs?

2. Do I center my thoughts around the activities of the abuser and the problems caused by that abuse?

3. Am I often disappointed by the promises that this family member has made and then broken?

4. Do I tend to avoid discussing my concerns and worries to avoid making matters worse?

5. Have I ever marked, hid, diluted, or emptied bottles of liquor, or hid drugs or medication?

6. Do I assume responsibility for the duties and

chores of my chemically dependent family member?

7. Have I withdrawn from friends and outside activities because I am embarrassed by the behavior of the addicted person in my life?

8. Do I experience physical symptoms like nausea, a knot in my stomach, body aches, headaches, depression, anxiety, panic, light-headedness?

9. When things get really bad, have I considered suicide? Or wished my loved one were dead?

10. Have I drunk excessively and abused medications myself to fit in—or to avoid the depression, anger, and loneliness brought on by the suffering in my family?

11. Have I experienced sexual problems, including feelings of revulsion, or avoided sex in response to the chemically dependent person's behavior?

12. Have I or other members of my family ever taken sides in a conflict or argument about the alcohol/drug abuser?

13. Have I or other members of my family shown signs of emotional stress, such as declining school or work performance, withdrawing from friends or family, having trouble with authority figures, having trouble in intimate relationships, or acting out sexually?

14. Have I thought everything would be O.K. if only the alcohol/drug abuser would stop or control the drinking or drug use?

15.. Have I or other members of my family experienced verbal, physical, or sexual abuse from an alcohol/drug abuser?

16. Have I or other members of my family experienced prolonged periods of depression or anxiety heightened by worry, shame, guilt, self-pity, anger, or resentment concerning the alcohol/drug abuser?

If you answered yes to just three of these questions, you should know more about AFMS.

Q: Why should I be concerned about AFMS?

A: Left untreated, AFMS has physical, emotional, and spiritual ramifications.

Affected family members often develop stress-related illnesses, high blood pressure, stomach ulcers, diarrhea, constipation, tremulousness, and other conditions. There is also evidence that links

Affected Family Member Syndrome with such disorders as anorexia nervosa and bulimia, phobias (including agoraphobia), workaholism, and in some cases, premenstrual syndrome.

In addition, AFMS exacts a marked emotional toll. This results in personal, social, and recreational difficulties as the *intoxicant emotions*—guilt, shame, self-pity, resentment, anger, and worry—exert an increasing influence on the affected family member. Communication and family breakdowns can occur.

Many affected family members are at a higher risk to marry a chemically dependent person or become chemically dependent themselves. Statistics show that about one-third of affected family members abuse alcohol or drugs to the point of dependency.

Q: Can Affected Family Member Syndrome or codependency apply to situations other than chemical dependency?

A: Yes, the term has broad application to any family in dysfunction. The California Model allows for four major categories contributing to family dysfunction. They are 1) addiction, 2) life crises, 3) mental illness, and 4) dysfunctional work setting. Co-alcoholics, codependents, adult children of alcoholics, and adolescents or children of alcoholics are all affected family members. The terms *co-alcoholic* and *codependent* were first used for the spouse of a chemically dependent person. However, anyone who puts the needs of others above his or her own needs in a self-defeating manner, allowing addictions or other problems to flourish and the relationship to become sick, is referred to as codependent. This could be a parent, an employer, a sibling, a friend.

All of these kinds of affected family members deserve special consideration and treatment.

Q: What is an "intoxicant emotion" example?

A: Intoxicant emotions are intense, un-expressed feelings of shame, anger, guilt, self-pity, resentment, and worry. Focusing on these emotions—becoming "intoxicated" with them—helps the affected family member cope with stress and alleviate emotional pain. However, affected family members are often unaware of this "coping" behavior and are likely to deny using intoxicant emotions.

We have thousands of feelings each day. When they are not expressed, feelings can become powerful emotions. Emotions left unexpressed over long periods have a negative physical, psychological, and spiritual impact. Affected Family Member Syndrome is truly a caring person's illness. So much emotional energy has been targeted to fixing the family that it becomes stored and unhealthy.

Even if affected family members do not take external chemicals, such as alcohol or other drugs, their own form of "chemical dependence" occurs from the stress chemicals manufactured by the body.

Remember that the body naturally manufactures many different kinds of chemicals. We are electro-chemical factories. The body chemical factory is capable of producing substances one thousand times more powerful than heroin. Repeated stress, as experienced by affected family members, can decrease the body's ability to produce healing chemicals and overproduce chemicals that promote illness.

A family member's strong, fight-or-flight response to

the stress caused by the difficult and unpredictable behavior of a chemically dependent person can create chemical and physical changes. Blood pressure rises. Heart rate and breathing become faster. The adrenal glands become more active. And changes in the gastro-intestinal tract and shifting of blood supply take place.

For defense, the family members unknowingly attempt to temper their stress by channeling it into the intoxicant emotions of shame, anger, guilt, self-pity, resentment, and worry. For a while, the stress thus becomes more manageable and easier to comprehend. It becomes something the affected family member can control to keep from facing the unpleasant realities of the loved one's addiction. This is reinforced with repetitive attempts to lessen or avoid the family problems. Some examples of this kind of repetitive behavior include sugarcoating the family problems for other people; avoiding discussing problems with family members or having volatile, fruitless discussions; and overcontrolling the behavior of the addict.

At this point, most of the emotions and behaviors are understandable and even healthy responses to short-term problems. However, the problems are usually *not* short term. This is a major fact that family members miss. They think they are preparing for a sprint when they're really getting ready for a marathon. Affected family members often learn this too late.

Eventually, the use of intoxicating emotions gets out of control and progresses, regardless of the addict's recovery status or his or her continued physical presence in the family. As time goes on, with snowballing of unexpressed feelings, these chemicals build in the body. Feelings and chemicals both lodge in the body and have a toxic effect. The affected family member requires less and less actual stress at home to experience the negative, toxic effects of the disease—just as an alcoholic or drug user eventually needs less and less of his chemical to produce intoxicating effects because of the buildup of substances in the body and the physical deterioration of body tissue and organs.

The major impact of the family stress, at least 70 percent of it, comes from the tremendous ability of human beings to anticipate all kinds of disasters. This anticipatory stress weakens, irritates, and defeats the affected family member even before the behavior of the chemically dependent person can provoke real stress. You will never see a rabbit become sick and paralyzed from worry over the upcoming hunting season. But we human beings can become sick and immobilized from anticipating problems.

Each time an affected family member engages in one of the intoxicant emotions, it is like picking up a bottle marked "Worry" or a needle labeled "Shame," "Guilt," "Self-pity," "Anger," or "Resentment." Hypothetically speaking, these emotions pack a punch similar to that of alcohol or other drugs.

Unfortunately, when family members become "intoxicated" by their own behaviors and emotions, it is difficult, if not impossible, for them to offer the kind of help their family really needs. One sad statistic that indicates this is the fact that 30 percent of adult children of alcoholics report being hurt more by their nondrinking parent.

Intoxicant emotions quite literally make affected family members drunk with the very worst aspects of their lives. The stress of trying to cope, to deny reality, to attempt to normalize the situation, to desperately keep everything from falling apart actually enables the family illness to progress.

Once people begin to understand that Affected Family Member Syndrome is a physically driven illness related to, but separate from, the chemical dependency of the loved one whose behavior is tearing the family apart, they are willing to hear that each family member needs to focus on his or her own self-recovery. The focal point of recovery changes from *you* have a problem, to *we* have a disease, to *I* have a disease.

Q: What is the progression of Affected Family Member Syndrome?

A: Some individuals use guilt, shame, anger, self-pity, worry, and resentment in their daily functioning. I call them emotional addicts. These persons are particularly vulnerable to AFMS. They find it difficult to cope with the inconsistent and disruptive behavior of an addict without falling back on the intoxicant emotions they are already used to using.

However, no matter what family members are like in the beginning, once chemical dependency envelops a family, no member is left unscarred. Most family members will progress into some symptoms of AFMS, and many will eventually require professional treatment.

The symptoms of AFMS are best understood in four phases. Remember that AFMS begins out of love. It is a perfectly normal response to be stressed and emotionally upset by watching someone you love sink into addiction. The first two phases of the disease represent that normal response. Phases Three and Four are more indicative of pathology and a physically driven condition.

It is important to remember that recovery can occur at any stage. *Family members should not wait until they have reached Phase Four in the progression to seek help.*

Phase One: Concern Phase

Initially, a family member will unknowingly use the intoxicant emotions (IE) occasionally as a natural reaction to a threat, as a false sense of security, or as an explanation of why life has become so stressful.

However, despite the increasingly negative behavior of the chemically dependent, the family member develops an increased tolerance for the chemically dependent's behavior. The family member also develops an increased tolerance for the presence in his/her own body of stress-related chemical changes.

Occasional use of the intoxicant emotions progresses to frequent and then constant use as the chemically dependent person's behavior causes pain and confusion for the family member.

In this phase, family members hold back from confronting the chemically dependent in order to avoid making matters worse and increasing the embarrassment of the family. Attempts to drink alcohol or use drugs to "keep up" with their loved one only worsen the situation.

The first *blockout* on the part of the affected family member may soon occur. When a spouse, child, or sibling literally cannot recall a recent, unpleasant incident caused by the chemically dependent's behavior, it marks the progression of the disease to Phase Two.

Phase Two: Defense Phase

As the affected family member's disease builds, blockouts of unpleasant evenings or occurrences become more frequent. There is a denial that anything in the family is going wrong. Roles are often traded or reversed. It is not unusual for children to take on the role of parent. Some children of chemically dependent persons appear to have skipped childhood.

A clustering of symptoms in Phase Two may also be observed, which include covering up the intoxicant emotions and pretending to others that everything is okay. The family member will also "protect" the chemically dependent person from the consequences of alcohol or drug abuse by making excuses, covering for him or her at work, lying to friends, or taking on some of his or her personal or financial responsibilities. The less control affected family members feel they have over the chemically dependent and themselves, the more they increase their efforts to control.

During Phase Two, affected family members may also express guilt for the chemically dependent's behavior—if they could be "better," more loving, help out more, and so forth, the chemically dependent person wouldn't drink/use as much.

At this stage, the affected family member still seems to be in control of the intoxicant emotions. However, in Phase Three, this control becomes lost and the negative behavior of the affected family member becomes increasingly apparent to other family members and friends.

Phase Three: Adaptation Phase

In Phase Three, the family member's life begins to revolve around the chemically dependent. All thoughts, actions, and decisions are centered on the chemically dependent's behavior. All matters become secondary to the needs and situation of the chemically dependent. It is at this phase that the illness becomes *physically* driven.

Affected family members begin to isolate themselves from others. Even close friends are avoided. Children, already embarrassed by the chemically dependent's behavior, become even more reluctant to bring friends home.

In Phase Three, affected family members continually maintain alibis for the chemically dependent's behavior and the family's difficulties. Symptoms worsen. Family members begin to demonstrate troubled behaviors. Children may run away from home or refuse to go to school. Spouses engage in self-deprivation and withdraw from social activities or any kind of fun. Or, at times, they may go to the other extreme and try to become "super-together" and "totally involved" in attempts to control or make amends for the family's situation. They try to be perfect.

However, the affected family member gradually begins to lose control over the IE—shame, guilt, resentment, self-pity, anger, and worry—just as the chemically dependent person experiences a progressive loss of control over alcohol or other drug use.

In this stage, the family member may become

aggressive, or return verbal or physical abuse to the chemically dependent person and others. Remorse is quite common, as the family member adapts to a negative way of life. Extreme loneliness and hopelessness set in.

Often, the affected family member's behavior becomes more distasteful to others than the behavior of the addict. Ironically, children may see the affected family member as *causing* the addict's alcohol or drug use. Affected family members develop marked self-pity because of their mis-understood role in the disruption, and at times, wonder if they are going insane. Affected family members often expend incredible energy to help others while neglecting themselves.

Physical escape or a change of friends, work, or home environment bring little relief. As the resentments become intolerable for the family member, a family breakdown occurs. Many breakdowns do not involve separation or divorce. Instead, the communication within the family becomes nonproductive. The family becomes stuck as the behavior of the chemically dependent person's affected family member deteriorates.

Affected family members often say they feel like the "living dead." They continue to function, but have no hope or joy in their lives. They may attempt to use alcohol or other drugs to keep up or fit in with their loved one's chemical use. Typically, affected family members eventually quit using alcohol and drugs entirely or also progress into dependency.

At this time, the affected family member may seek help for medical or psychological problems. There is an increased danger of prescription drug dependency for family members who obtain legal, mood-altering chemicals. Often, Affected Family Member Syndrome is misinterpreted as a primary depressive or anxiety state or as an adjustment or personality disorder.

The family member continues to suffer from feelings of failure and low self-esteem, which catapults him or her into the exhaustion phase of affected family syndrome.

Phase Four: Exhaustion Phase

In Phase Four, the affected family member experiences "binges" on the intoxicant emotions. These emotional binges are similar to the binges or "benders" which occur in the chronic phase of chemical dependency.

The periods of time in which the affected family member spends in the intoxicant emotions become more extended in Phase Four. IE-induced states of depression or anxiety last for weeks or months.

Some last attempts to "fix" the family or unknowingly defend the IE abuse to others are made by affected family members prior to surrendering to a total loss of self-worth. Even the chemically dependent person's recovery can fail to restore the affected family member's self-esteem and lowered stress tolerance. Now, just a small dose of stress or IE results in physical, spiritual, and psychological deterioration.

The affected family member, if not helped, will continue to become physically, emotionally, and spiritually bankrupt. Tremors and fears, along with the now obsessive use of IE, precede a desperate need for a spiritual base.

The affected family member, while still maintaining a facade of normalcy, sees no way out and feels out of control. No rationalization can compensate for the obvious deterioration. At this point, the affected family member is faced with the same options as the chronic chemically dependent person: recovery and abstinence from the intoxicant emotions, insanity, or death. (To help you review, a summary of the progression of AFMS is presented in chart form on pages 50-51.)

Q: I have a chemically dependent person in my family. I have tried to avoid the intoxicant emotions and have practiced a "tough love" approach. Do I still have AFMS?

A: Yes. The emotional and physical stress of the situation cannot be willed away. Like chemical dependency, AFMS can be likened to a vulture sitting on your shoulder; you can't get rid of it, but you can prevent it from eating you up. The more actively you participate in recovery programs like Al-Anon, the smaller the vulture and its impact. The less active the recovery program, the larger and more damaging the vulture becomes.

Q: Can you explain more about family roles in Affected Family Member Syndrome?

A: The concept of birth order having an effect on family roles was first developed by Alfred

Adler, M.D., and people like Sharon Wegscheider-Cruse, Claudia Black, and Janet Woititz have over the past few years popularized the idea that people in chemically dependent families tend to act out certain roles that help them cope with emotional stress.

The popularized roles are as follows:

Spouse or Parent

The *chief enabler* is the person with the most to lose if the relationship fails. He or she exhibits a tremendous denial of reality and, in an attempt to normalize the situation, tries to become increasingly responsible and controlling which can enable the illness to progress.

First-born

The family *prince* or *hero* assumes an overresponsible, I-will-fix-it role. The first-born strives to keep the family intact while directing energy to overachievement outside the home.

Middle Children

Middle children often assume roles not taken by the first-born, often producing the exact opposite behavior.

The *scapegoat* acts out the family's hidden conflicts.

This individual sees roles in the family as limited and chooses not to invest much time in the family. Peers are looked to for support and the acceptance of that group becomes of primary concern.

The *lost child* turns inward for validation as the family problems increase. Daydreams and fantasies fulfill a need to feel accepted and adequate.

Last Born

The *mascot:* The family pet is frequently found in the last born ordinal position. They tend to be humorous and charming and add a light touch to difficult situations. Their intense anxiety and fear is often overlooked as their disposition is so comforting and pleasant.

It is important to note that many factors go into a family's make-up, and birth-order roles may be reversed. In addition, Dr. Adler emphasized that siblings who are more than five years apart may not view each other as siblings. For example, the youngest child may tend to view the oldest child as another adult.

Family roles, sibling rivalry, and competition for recognition and acceptance do not stop once the family grows up. Usually the patterns continue. Therefore, it is more usual for family members to have divided opinions on what is occurring in the family, specifically whether or not one of the family members is an alcoholic or drug addict. Realizing that you are unconsciously acting in a particular fixed pattern or role in relation to those around you is a good first step in stopping those behaviors if they are harmful.

Q: What can be done about AFMS?

A: Just as total abstinence from alcohol or drugs is the basis for a chemically dependent person's recovery, total abstinence from the intoxicant emotions—guilt, shame, anger, self-pity, worry, and resentment—is the basis of recovery for an affected family member.

Affected family members need to learn to laugh and have fun. Recreation and leisure activities are vital. Life should not revolve around the chemically dependent person's past or present behavior.

As an affected family member, you should seriously consider joining a self-help group like Al-Anon or Alateen. Such groups are based on the

Twelve Steps of Alcoholics Anonymous, but have been adapted for family members of chemically dependent people. They provide vital components of recovery, including fellowship with people who have similar problems, encouragement in living life one day at a time and in developing the spiritual (not religious) parts of ourselves. Self-help groups offer some of the most rewarding, effective, and fun ways to approach life. However, most affected family members—especially men—do not make use of these groups. Unfamiliarity with and distrust of the groups, lack of time, and denial ("The alcoholic needs to change but I don't") often keep affected family members from joining self-help groups.

Family members need to accept help from others, the same help they unselfishly gave to others. Self-help group meetings are available in nearly every city in the United States, and the main offices are listed in the yellow pages of the phone book.

In addition, professional treatment programs continue to offer comprehensive workshops and counseling opportunities to assist the affected family member in recovery. Family members have an equal need for and right to treatment offered to chemically dependent persons, *whether or not the chemically dependent is in treatment.*

Right now, you might feel that it would be impossible for you to abandon the intoxicant emotions. After all, you can't stop thoughts or feelings from entering your mind. It's true that none of us can prevent a fleeting thought. But affected family members actually "binge" on intoxicant emotions for hours, days, weeks, months, and even years. It is this kind of behavior that you must abstain from.

Your treatment counselor can help you examine which intoxicant emotions your body has been conditioned to "abuse," and how often and in what ways you abused them. Your counselor also will help you build a support network and develop healthier coping skills. For example, you might feel certain emotions coming on and think something like, I can tell I'm going to spend the whole weekend really upset and resentful. Call your counselor, your self-help group sponsor or fellow members, or other members of the support network. They will help you recenter and remember that you cannot really afford even one more "binge."

Family members are encouraged not to make any major life changes—such as divorce, a move, or a career change—in their first year of recovery. AFMS is a disease which, like chemical dependency, takes months and years to progress. Recovery, too, takes time. Recovery is a process, but from the beginning of treatment, you will feel better. Even if things appear to become temporarily worse, your outlook will improve.

If you can identify the early phases of AFMS in yourself, seek help from a professional in the chemical dependency field. The sooner you start, the better your chances of success.

Q: While I am in treatment myself, should I try to get the addict in my family into treatment?

A: As the family member of a chemically dependent person, you are probably familiar with the term *intervention*. But let's look at a different kind of intervention: one that focuses on you, the affected family member.

There are three kinds of intervention. The first is crisis-driven. For example, your loved one has an accident while driving, is fired from a job, or is hospitalized. During the crisis, a judge, a doctor, or family members insist that the chemically dependent person get help.

The second kind of intervention is induced-crisis intervention. Family members and a professional therapist *confront* the chemically dependent person with the evidence that he or she needs help and ask him or her to enter treatment before a more serious crisis can occur.

The third kind of intervention is the "support technique" of intervention. *The goal of the support technique is to encourage the most motivated member of the family to seek assessment or treatment first.* This kind of intervention harmonizes with the Al-Anon principle that you, the affected family member, must attend to your own recovery and stop trying to "fix" the drinking/using of your loved one.

Your first steps in practicing the support technique of intervention and in beginning your own recovery are exactly the same. You must seek help from a professional chemical dependency counselor, have an assessment, and initiate an individualized treatment program. Choose a treatment center or therapist that is familiar with chemical dependency, codependency, and intervention. Through regular counseling and role play, you can learn about your illness and learn how your behavior has helped prevent communication in the family. Role play often reveals that chemical abuse in the family is avoided as a topic, or that when it is discussed, the talks are irrational and highly emotional.

Sometime in about the first two months of your treatment, your counselor will invite the chemically dependent person in your family to provide input into *your* recovery. During this first joint session, the focus is predominantly on *you*, the affected family member. The tone of the meeting should be warm, open, and very matter-of-fact. The topic under discussion is your illness and your treatment plan. The chemically dependent person's drinking/drug history is discussed as a concern of yours, but direct confrontation of the chemically dependent person should be avoided.

Most often, what happens in this session is that the affected family member shares his or her concerns, and the addict denies having any problem with alcohol or other drugs. This expected conflict can be resolved by the counselor, who offers to do an assessment for the addict at another time. This usually occurs at the end of the session and is offered as a solution to a central conflict. If the addict is not willing to undergo a drinking/drug-use assessment, the counselor invites him or her to participate once a month in the affected family member's treatment, by providing input and reporting on any progress.

Again, at all times, the primary focus is on assisting the affected family member and discussing how the affected family member feels the family is coping, *not* on the chemically dependent person. The chemically dependent person *cooperates* in the affected family member's treatment, *observes* the positive changes, and is *invited*—not confronted—to undergo a drinking/drug-use assessment.

Years of clinical experience with this intervention technique have shown that, during this process, the chemically dependent person usually becomes more trusting and accepting of treatment for him- or herself. Additionally, others in the family, including the addict, begin to model the positive behavior the affected family member has learned in treatment and will often seek help as well. In my experience, very few addicts are unwilling to give input into their loved one's counseling. However, they *are* often unwilling to be confronted by their loved ones or by a therapist.

A word of caution: the affected family member must be truly committed to his or her own recovery. The support technique doesn't work when family members try to use it as a "ruse" to lure an addict into treatment. *Better to concentrate on your own treatment if you feel unprepared or uncertain about bringing the addict in your life into the recovery process.*

The following case study provides a glimpse of a typical affected family member's experience with the support technique.

The Case of Mary M.

Mary M. was an attractive woman in her early forties, married with two preteenage children. She worked as a teacher and volunteered frequently at a local church.

Mary often felt nervous and, for no apparent reason, panicky. She felt her children did not respect her and frequently fought with them. She deeply resented her husband's heavy drinking and cocaine use, but she never shared these feelings with anyone. She had stopped both drinking and using cocaine three years ago, but she felt guilty for ever having used drugs.

One day in the classroom, Mary began weeping openly. What kept running through her mind was that she was not a good person.

Soon after, she heard a radio talk show about Affected Family Member Syndrome. A friend suggested that Mary was suffering from this illness. Mary immediately denied this possibility and defended the way she had dealt with her family.

Later, however, she decided to call and talk to a counselor at a local chemical dependency center. After listening for a while to her family history, the counselor suggested that Mary's husband was chemically dependent, and that possibly her father had been an alcoholic. He encouraged Mary to join Al-Anon.

In Al-Anon and in a therapy group for affected family members, Mary began to see the many ways AFMS had impacted upon her life. She recognized that her perfectionism and work-aholism were aspects of her illness.

Mary's husband was asked to participate in several sessions to give input into her recovery. At first, he denied that he had a problem, but, as he became familiar and comfortable with the counseling process, he began to talk about his drinking and drug use. Eventually, he accepted treatment for his own chemical dependency.

Later, their children were assessed, and it was found that they, too, were affected by the family problems. Their daughter had an eating disorder and their son had begun to experiment with drugs at school. Both children joined Alateen and began their own education about chemical dependency and AFMS. Clearly, they were a family with a lot of work to do, but things were looking up. Each knew that successfully working together as a family also meant paying attention to his or her own individualized recovery program.

Q: What is the recovery process of AFMS or codependency?

A: Just as the family member's illness parallels the progression of chemical dependency, so too does the recovery process of family members parallel that of the addict.

We can think of recovery in three phases: (1) prelapse, (2) true recovery, and (3) relapse prevention and quality life change.

Q: What is prelapse?

A: Prelapse is the first phase of the recovery process. It is a transition period when family members struggle to accept that alcohol and drugs are a primary problem. A time when they need to work their own recovery program to keep from being further affected by this family disease.

It's possible to get stuck in the prelapse stage. The family member may recognize the problem and participate in a recovery program, but never achieve true recovery. Before defining true recovery, let's look at the typical progression of prelapse. Not everyone goes through the stages of prelapse in this order, but the appearance of these signs and symptoms in clusters is a good sign that a person is moving toward recovery. However, it is also a warning. The individual needs to commit to true recovery to stop the downward spiral of AFMS.

Prelapse Symptoms

The affected family member:

1. Has the first painful realizations that family and life problems are related to his or her own behavior, not just the behavior of the addict in the family.

2. Recognizes the loss or pulling away of friends and family, but chooses not to deal with it.

3. Makes serious attempts to alter or control escalating negative emotions—self-pity, guilt, resentment, worry, anger, shame. Examples: smiling and acting perfect to hide feelings; projecting feelings onto others, including the chemically dependent person; overcompensating for feelings of hurt and unworthiness by overcontrolling self and others.

4. Becomes upset over deteriorating relationships.

5. Rationalizes and justifies the need to keep problems secret, bottle up emotions, and deny self-needs, despite increasingly serious psychological and medical consequences.

6. Gets annoyed with others' awareness of his or her stress and physical, psychological, and spiritual losses.

7. Makes initial attempts to alter drastically her or his negative emotional state.

8. Is disturbed by deteriorating mental, physical, and spiritual health.

9. Is aware that this deteriorating state alters his or her relationships in a negative way.

10. Experiences escalating life problems.

11. Has fantasy wishes to be nurtured, rescued, and made safe. Has similar wishes for all family members.

12. Identifies life crises as resulting from his or her rigid, compulsive behavior.

13. Fails at constant attempts to control self and others.

14. Finds exhaustion overwhelming.

15. Seeks help for deteriorating condition.

16. Works towards true recovery.

When a person is seeking help for AFMS, but cannot yet commit to true recovery, often his or her efforts are overshadowed by what I call "prelapse secrets." A few examples of prelapse secrets are presented below.

• **Covering up.** The affected family member doesn't disclose the full history of the family's problems with chemicals, verbal and/or physical abuse, financial trouble, incest, or other problems.

• **Setting a date.** The affected family member accepts help only to see if the change works by a certain time. When it doesn't, the family member goes back to the old lifestyle.

• **Believing, "I am different."** "Our family's not as bad off as *those* people."

• **Saying, "No doubt. However. . . ."** "*No doubt*

my loved one is an alcoholic/addict. *However*, at least I have someone I can relate to and feel connected to. I don't want to rock the boat."

"*No doubt* we have serious problems in our family. *However*, to try to change things would create a more serious crisis that I'm not prepared for."

• **Denying physical impairment.** Affected family members often appear more physically and mentally stable than they really are. Their verbal skills and denial can mask potentially serious medical or neurological pathology. If unrecognized and untreated, this can detract from the benefits of treatment and keep family members in pre-recovery—stuck in prelapse. For example, affected family members have an increased risk of heart disease. They often suffer severe, stress-related headaches and back pain that heighten their irritability and make them combative with their chemically dependent loved one. Their inability to think clearly may even make it unsafe for them to drive automobiles. There's an old joke that came from affected-family groups in my treatment center: half of all accidents are caused by alcoholics; the other half are caused by their family members.

Q: What is true recovery?

A: True recovery is the second phase of the recovery process. If intervention in the prelapse stage occurs, denial patterns are lessened. And the family becomes willing to work on self. As the "Big Book" of AA states, "Half measures availed us nothing." Half measures in recovery result in half efforts that keep us half-ill. Lasting recovery requires a full commitment to true recovery. AFMS in the advanced phases must be treated as a serious medical illness. True recovery from this disease means developing a happy lifestyle— allowing fun into your life. It also requires meeting most of the following criteria:

1. Total abstinence from all intoxicant emotions and behaviors for *at least* ninety days, and a sincere desire to maintain *ongoing* abstinence from all intoxicating emotions and behaviors.

2. The return of physical, emotional, and spiritual health.

3. Increasing ability to relax, identify and meet self-needs, and enjoy frequent laughter.

4. A willingness to cooperate in an individualized

treatment plan and/or appropriate self-help group(s) based on the Twelve Steps and Twelve Traditions of AA, including:

a. Finding and working with a sponsor.
b. Attending several meetings weekly and having at least one "home group" (a meeting you attend every week); ninety meetings in ninety days, especially early in recovery, is highly recommended.
c. Daily readings and meditation.
d. Completing thorough Fourth and Fifth Steps.*
e. Daily review of prelapse and recovery symptoms.

Remember, these criteria should serve as *minimum* expectations of true recovery. Achieving true recovery should never be interpreted as being able to return to your former stressful, compulsive lifestyle. Again, many individuals never pass through the prelapse phase into true recovery. Early recovery requires careful adherence to the above criteria to ensure that the first two phases of recovery—prelapse and true recovery—are

AA's Fourth Step is, "Made a searching and fearless moral inventory of ourselves." The Fifth Step is, "Admitted to God, to ourselves, and to another human being the exact nature of our wrongs."

achieved, before focusing on the third phase: quality life change and relapse prevention.

Q: You said earlier that people suffering from AFMS have a strong tendency to relapse. What does this mean?

A: Relapse is a pattern of attitudes, thoughts, feelings, emotions, and behaviors that leads to a resumption of intoxicant emotions and compulsivity, after true recovery has been achieved. All relapses are planned, but the individual is often unaware of the pattern developing.

Affected family members who relapse into old patterns of thoughts, feelings, behavior, and physical stress not only suffer self-injury but can harm other family members and add stress to the person recovering from chemical dependency.

However, the majority of affected family members never achieve true recovery and are in a state of prelapse, not relapse. That is, they never surrender to the reality that *they* have a problem that requires treatment.

Once you have achieved true recovery, remember that the "vulture" is still sitting on your shoulder; your counselor and self-help groups can help you make an individualized plan for ongoing relapse prevention.

Q: What are some practical ways for affected family members to reduce stress?

A: Here is a twelve point plan for stress management for affected family members:

1. As the First Step of Alcoholics Anonymous recommends: Admit you are powerless over alcohol, drugs, and/or your loved one, and that your life has become unmanageable. Accept your illness. You have a disease. It is called Affected Family Member Syndrome.

2. As much as you can, abstain from the intoxicant emotions—guilt, worry, shame, resentment, self-pity, and anger.

3. Attend Al-Anon, Nar-Anon, Alateen, Coda, or other self-help group meetings.

4. Eat properly, get at least eight hours of sleep per night, and exercise regularly (at least three days per week for a minimum of twenty minutes each time).

5. Abstain from or at least decrease your intake of the societally approved, stress-inducing drugs: caffeine in coffee, tea, and soft drinks; nicotine in cigarettes and cigars; and ethanol in alcoholic beverages, to mention a few.

6. You become what you think about most of the time, so:

   a. Think positively.
   b. Compliment yourself often.
   c. "Psych" yourself up—meet challenges.
   d. Don't make boring, negative statements about yourself.
   e. Channel your tensions into productivity.

7. Try spontaneity—stop controlling yourself, the world, and others. Stop planning, plotting, and preparing. Enjoy yourself and your life one minute at a time.

8. Get out with friends (or just yourself) and have fun. Make your recreation and leisure time a high priority. There is a saying in the AA Program: "Stick with the winners." Avoid people who will worsen your mood.

9. Develop the ability to laugh at yourself and your problems. Don't be so serious all the time.

10. To feel like a comfortable, happy person, you must first act like one. Treat others as you would have them treat you.

11. Work your own program of recovery, no one else's.

12. Don't wait for your life goals to be achieved before you're happy. Remember the saying, "Happiness is found along the way, not at the end of the journey."

Summary

There is an illness that is related to, but separate from, the disease of chemical dependency. I call the illness of affected family members Affected Family Member Syndrome or AFMS. AFMS in the later phases of the illness is a physically driven disease; it is driven by a dependency on chemicals produced within the human body. These are the "fight or flight" chemicals we all have. AFMS is not a moral deficiency, personality disorder, or a mental illness.

When these chemicals build up within the body, the individual copes with them by channeling the stress into certain emotions—guilt, shame, self-pity, anger, resentment, and worry. Gradually, as more and more long-term stress is experienced, the individual becomes "intoxicated" with these emotions, i.e., uses them as an automatic protection from stress. Soon, the presence of these chemicals in the body is driving the behavior of the person; very little actual stress is needed to produce them. A person suffering from this illness has a compulsive need to control him- or herself and others. He or she experiences an array of stress-related physical symptoms like high blood pressure, ulcers, and headaches.

AFMS is a highly treatable disease that parallels the progression and recovery symptoms of chemical dependency. However, intervention and treatment are not as widely prescribed for affected family members as for chemically dependent people. This is particularly tragic when we consider that 60 percent of chemically dependent persons are *also* affected family members, and a lesser percentage are suffering from Fetal Alcohol Syndrome. People with such a "blended" diagnosis are much more difficult to treat. However, treatment is available and should be actively sought. Membership in a self-help group like Al-Anon or Coda should be part of the treatment program. The affected family member's best bet for keeping focused on his or her own recovery, while helping a chemically dependent loved one, is the support technique of intervention.

Those people who have gotten help for AFMS sometimes say that they are actually grateful for having this disease. Otherwise they might never have learned how to live a serene, comfortable, spiritually enlightened life. This kind of life, that contains one precious moment after another, is what I like to call "recovery plus." Recovery plus is available to you, too. Show yourself the same care and concern that you have shown your chemically dependent loved one.

CALIFORNIA MODEL FOR ADDICTION RECOVERY (CMAR)

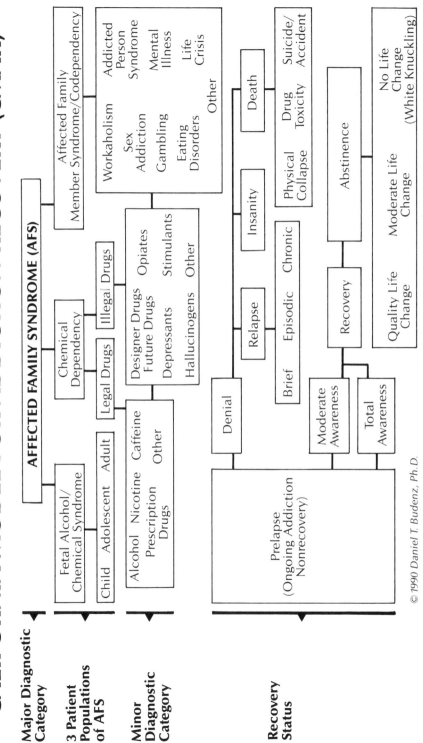

© 1990 Daniel T. Budenz, Ph.D.

AFFECTED FAMILY MEMBER SYNDROME
(AFMS, also called codependency)

Concurrent Symptoms in the Progression of Family Illness

I: CONCERN PHASE

1. Concern for the loved one (Occasional use of IE)
2. Denial of the problem (Frequent use of IE)
3. Increased tolerance for chemically dependent's negative behavior and for IE

4. ——— FIRST BLOCKOUT

II: DEFENSE PHASE

5. Covering up IE
6. Preoccupation with chemically dependent
7. Protecting the chemically dependent
8. High tolerance for inappropriate behavior
9. Feels responsible for all family problems
10. Repeated blockouts

11. ——— LOSS OF IE CONTROL

III: ADAPTATION PHASE

12. Guilt and embarrassment
13. Perfect-person behavior
14. Marked anger
15. Increased alcohol/drug consumption by family member
16. Remorse and stress
17. Adapts to uncomfortable way of life
18. Chemically-dependent-centered behavior
19. Tendencies toward isolation and/or over involvement

The Intoxicant Emotions (IE) are shame, guilt, resentment, self-pity, worry, and anger.

These emotions unknowingly become a "high" or coping mechanism for the persons close to the chemically dependent. Family members select their intoxicant emotions just as the chemically dependent selects alcohol or other drugs.

20. Marked self-pity or shame
21. Gives too much to others, nothing for self
22. Resentments become intolerable
23. Absent mindedness
24. Family breakdown
25. Medical or psychological care
26. Feelings of failure
27. Diminished self-esteem

28. _____ "BENDERS"/BINGES ON IE

IV: EXHAUSTION PHASE

29. Defending use of IE
30. Total loss of self-worth
31. Loss of tolerance for chemically dependent and IE
32. Deterioration
33. Tremors and fears
34. Marked anxiety and/or depression
35. Spiritual need
36. Rationalizations fail

| ADMISSION AND RECOVERY | OR | INSANITY OR DEATH |

RECOVERY PROCESS

Recovery can occur at any point in the progression.

The earlier the illness is arrested, the better the chances of recovery.

Binges on Intoxicant Emotions Stop

Self-recovery Becomes Priority

Emotional Detachment from the Chemically Dependent

Physical, Spiritual, Emotional Health Returns

Desire to Continue Recovery

Recommended Reading

Beattie, Melody. *Codependent No More.* Center City, Minnesota: Hazelden, 1987.

Beattie, Melody. *Beyond Codependency.* New York: Harper and Row, 1989.

Black, Claudia. *It Will Never Happen to Me.* Denver: MAC Publishing, 1982.

Budenz, Daniel T., Ph.D., C.A.D.C. *Prelapse, Relapse, and True Recovery.* Minneapolis: CompCare Publishers, 1990.

Wegscheider-Cruse, Sharon. *Choicemaking.* Deerfield Beach, Florida: Health Communications, 1985.

Whitfield, Charles L., M.D. *Healing the Child Within.* Deerfield Beach, Florida: Health Communications, 1987.

Woititz, Janet. *Adult Children of Alcoholics.* Deerfield Beach, Florida: Health Communications, 1983.

Wolter, Dwight Lee. *A Life Worth Waiting For!: For All Adult Children of Alcoholics, Messages from a Survivor.* Minneapolis: CompCare Publishers, 1989.

Wolter, Dwight Lee. *Forgiving Our Parents.* Minneapolis: CompCare Publishers, 1989.

Appendix

Fetal Alcohol Syndrome

Most people now know that a mother's drinking/ drug use during early pregnancy is harmful. Alcohol and other drugs cross the placenta to the fetus, causing complications that can include miscarriage, organ damage, brain damage, and growth and developmental retardation. Newborn FAS children show a lighter than normal birth weight, smaller head circumference, and altered facial features—lowered ears, small eyes, flattened profile, flat, elongated philtrum (space between nose and lip), and a thin upper lip. FAS children tend to have shorter attention spans, learning and motor disabilities, and any number of physical complications or complaints.

Adults with FAS (3 to 5 percent of the population) are very aware of their learning and physical problems, but often are unaware of their relation to FAS. A lowered self-esteem is an added concern for the FAS adult. They experience shame and embarrassment over their unexplained differences. Many FAS adults report being addicted from the first few drinking/drug experiences.

Chemical Dependency

The disease process and progression of alcohol and drug dependency is perhaps best summarized by an ancient Chinese saying:

> The man takes a drink.
> Then the drink takes a drink.
> Then the drink takes the man.

The chemically dependent person is one who over time needs to take more and more alcohol or other drugs but gets progressively less of the "positive effect" and more negative effects. The chemically dependent person experiences a change in physiology that, once consumption resumes, condemns him or her to eventual loss of control and an overwhelming preoccupation with and craving to continue using. Once the physiology is altered, there is no return to safe, controlled using. Total abstinence is the starting point to recovery from this life-threatening disease.

Chemical dependency is primarily a physically driven disease, resulting from one or more of the following:

1) a genetic condition
2) maternal consumption of alcohol or other drugs during pregnancy, that can cause babies to be addicted at birth (Fetal Alcohol Effects or Syn-

drome or affects of other chemicals on the fetus. I prefer the term fetal chemical effects or syndrome, which recognizes many legal and illegal drugs that are affecting our society.)

3) an individual's chronic, repititious use of alcohol or other drugs, progressing into addiction

Chemical dependency is rarely seen independent of a prior or subsequent addiction to alcohol or other drugs in the family.

Family members often become as physically, psychologically, and spiritually affected as the chemically dependent person and require similar intervention, treatment, and support services.

Recovery, both for the chemically dependent person and the affected family member, is characterized by three identifiable phases:

1) prelapse
2) true recovery
3) quality-of-life change, which includes prevention of relapse

Advances in genetics research continue to support observations by early pioneers in the alcoholism field that the disease runs in families. This suggests a hereditary influence in the development of addiction, as well as learned or environmental factors. Children of alcoholics adopted and raised by nonalcoholic families show up to a threefold increase in alcoholism over adopted children of nonalcoholics (Goodwin, 1971, and Bohman, 1981). Studies tracking the incidence of alcoholism in twin children of alcoholics showed a matching percentage, confirming the possibility of a hereditary trait. Research data on families and individuals provide additional evidence that alcoholism is not only a disease but one that is most likely inherited (Schuckit, 1984, and Gabrielli, 1982). Enzyme abnormalities in alcoholics first identified in Australia and recently confirmed in the United States are increasing the field's interest in genetics.

Future research with people who have Fetal Alcohol Syndrome may provide more insight into why so many individuals are so quickly addicted. Research efforts also are necessary to identify what is physically, and perhaps hereditarily, going on with persons suffering from Affected Family Member Syndrome or codependency. Henry Begleiter, M.D., Ph.D., of New York has found that adult children of alcoholics have identifiable brain wave patterns. However, we are probably at the same level of understanding about the disease process of AFMS as alcoholism researchers were when William D. Silkworth, M.D., first wrote his "Doctor's Opinion" about alcoholism in the "Big Book" of Alcoholics Anonymous fifty years ago.

About the Author

Daniel T. Budenz, Ph.D., C.A.D.C., has been a specialist in the chemical dependency field for over twenty years. Dr. Budenz developed the California Model—a model of disease process that underscores whole-family recovery. Dr. Budenz is chairman of the National Association for Affected Families (NAAF) and has established or directed chemical dependency centers in Illinois, Wisconsin, and California. He was the founder of the DePaul/Madison Family Institute in Madison, Wisconsin, and continues a portion of that clinic partnership with DePaul Hospital. Dr. Budenz is a member of the Alcohol/Drug Counselor Training Faculty at UCLA and was cofounder of the Southern California chapter for the National Association for Addiction Treatment Providers.

Dr. Budenz is an alumnus of the Betty Ford Center Professional in Residency (PIR) Program and an international consultant and lecturer. He is writing a book on family recovery, and recently completed a five-part videotape series, "The California Model."

Dr. Budenz lives with his wife Janice, daughter Kimberly, and son Thomas in Westlake Village, California.